CW01513041

Original title:

Echoes of the Phoenix's Heart

Author: Olivia Oja

ISBN HARDBACK: 978-1-80561-257-5

ISBN PAPERBACK: 978-1-80561-818-8

Voice of the Eternal Rebirth

In whispers soft, the world awakes,
The dawn brings hope, as silence breaks.
Nature's song begins to rise,
A testament beneath the skies.

With every breath, a story told,
Of dreams reborn and hearts of gold.
The past, a shimmer in the light,
Guiding souls through the night.

The seasons change, a steadfast call,
Through trial, we stumble, rise, and fall.
Yet in the cycle, wisdom found,
In every echo and every sound.

From ashes dark, new life emerges,
In quiet strength, the spirit surges.
A dance of time, forever spun,
In harmony, we are all one.

Flames that Dance in Shadows

In twilight's glow, the embers play,
A flickering light to guide the way.
Whispers twist in the cooling air,
Where shadows linger, bold and bare.

The fire's heart knows every fear,
Yet draws us in, we gather near.
Its warmth ignites both hope and pain,
In burning truths, we find the gain.

Each flicker tells of battles fought,
In fiery depths, lessons caught.
The dance of light, a timeless show,
As dreams ignite and embers glow.

In shadows deep, our spirits rise,
Embracing light through darkened skies.
For in the flame, both fierce and bright,
We find our strength, our guiding light.

Heartbeat of the Celestial Flame

Among the stars, a rhythm we hear,
A pulse that beats, both far and near.
Galaxies whisper, as time flows,
In cosmic ballet, the universe grows.

From stardust born, we rise and fall,
Connected deeply, one and all.
The heartbeat echoes, soft and strong,
A timeless lullaby, our song.

In every flicker, a life anew,
A tapestry woven, a vibrant hue.
Through shadowed realms, where light once shone,
In this vast dance, we are not alone.

The flame ignites with each heartbeat's grace,
Illuminating beauty in every place.
With hope unfurled, we reach for the sky,
Together we rise, we soar, we fly.

The Cycle of Fire and Flight

With wings unfurled, we rise in fire,
Chasing the dreams that take us higher.
Through storms we soar, through skies we glide,
In the dance of life, we find our stride.

The flames ignite the path we tread,
In every heartbeat, dreams are fed.
A cycle woven of light and shade,
In the embrace of night, our fears displayed.

From ashes cold, we take to the air,
With hopeful hearts, we cast our care.
For in the fire, transformation lies,
And in each flight, the spirit flies.

The winds will guide, the stars align,
In endless circles, we intertwine.
Through every rise and every fall,
The cycle continues, binding us all.

The Iridescent Flight

Wings of color soar so high,
Beneath a vast and open sky.
Whispers of dreams take to the air,
In a dance of freedom, bold and rare.

Clouds become the blanket soft,
Gentle breezes lift aloft.
Every hue tells a tale,
Of journeys taken, winds that sail.

Through twilight's glow, a vision bright,
Promises shimmer in the light.
With every flap, horizons change,
In the heart, beauty feels so strange.

Time suspended, moment divine,
In this flight, all souls align.
A symphony of colors blend,
As the world bends, and we transcend.

An iridescent path we tread,
In the sky where hopes are spread.
Freedom rings in every beat,
As we embrace the journey sweet.

Resilience in the Twilight

Beneath the stars, shadows creep,
Yet in the silence, dreams don't sleep.
Echoes of strength fill the night,
In the darkness, there's a light.

Whispers of hope linger near,
Carried on winds, strong and clear.
Roots grow deeper, reaching wide,
In every challenge, we abide.

Stars like embers in the deep,
Guard the secrets we wish to keep.
With every breath, we rise anew,
In twilight's hue, we find our view.

Seasons change, yet we hold fast,
Learning from the shadows cast.
With every trial, barriers break,
Finding strength in every ache.

Resilient hearts in twilight's grace,
Face the world, no fear to face.
Together, we embrace the dawn,
With spirits fierce, we carry on.

Vision Beyond the Flames

In the heart of embers, shadows dance,
Flickers of life in a fiery trance.
Glimmers of hope rise through despair,
With every spark, a tale laid bare.

What once was lost can be reclaimed,
In the heat, our souls unchained.
Visions of light break through the night,
Though surrounded, we seek the light.

Eyes that blaze with fervent fire,
Transforming pain into desire.
Through ashes gray, seeds of change grow,
In every heart, a warmth will show.

From darkness emerges hope anew,
In the blaze, we find what's true.
The heat ignites our bold intent,
In the flames, our spirits are lent.

Vision beyond the heat we bear,
In every flame, a dream laid bare.
Together we rise, no longer confined,
Transforming strife into the sublime.

The Phoenix's Soliloquy

Amidst the ashes, a whisper sings,
Of rebirth, of eternal springs.
A fiery heart beats strong and loud,
From the wreckage, a voice so proud.

Once bound by chains of yesterday,
Now soaring free, I find my way.
With every struggle, I ignite,
A journey vast, in the endless night.

Watch me rise, a silhouette bright,
Transforming shadows into light.
With wings adorned in flame's embrace,
I dance through time, I find my place.

Echoes of past in every feather,
A tapestry woven, stitched together.
I learn, I grow, I break the norm,
In the glow, I feel reborn.

The phoenix sings of all I've shed,
Of battles fought and tears I've bled.
In this soliloquy of flame,
I rise, unbowed, and claim my name.

Crimson Ascension

In the dawn, the skies unfold,
A tapestry of red and gold.
Hearts ablaze with fervent might,
Together we ascend the light.

Mountains high, we raise our gaze,
In the warmth of sunlight's blaze.
Colors dance in nature's song,
In this place, we all belong.

Rivers flow with passion's roar,
Braving waves, we seek to soar.
Hand in hand, we face the storm,
In unity, our hearts are warm.

Crimson threads weave tales of old,
Of dreams chased and stories told.
In shadows deep, our spirits rise,
A journey cloaked in endless skies.

With every breath, we claim our fate,
In the moment, we elevate.
The stars align, our spirits dance,
In this realm, we take our chance.

Resilient Spirit

In the face of trials, we stand,
With a fire ignited, hand in hand.
Each setback, a spark to ignite,
In darkness, we shall be the light.

Through the storms that shake our core,
We find strength to rise and soar.
Roots run deep, yet we still bend,
In our hearts, we shall not end.

Each wound tells a tale of grace,
In the mirror, we find our place.
With grit and love, we pave the way,
Our spirit shines, come what may.

In every challenge, seeds are sown,
Through the struggle, we have grown.
With a heart that never tires,
We ignite our inner fires.

Together, we will forge ahead,
In every thought, the light we spread.
Resilient souls, forever bold,
In this journey, we behold.

From Cinders to Light

From ashes cold, a spark will flare,
In the silence, we find our prayer.
With hope reborn, we rise anew,
A testament to courage true.

Once hidden deep, now flames ignite,
Cinder hearts glow soft and bright.
Through the shadows, we take our flight,
A dance of souls into the night.

Each flicker tells of battles won,
In the darkness, we find the sun.
With every breath, we breathe in life,
From cinders born, we conquer strife.

Winds of change, they lift our song,
In harmony, we all belong.
From the depths, our spirits soar,
In the light, we seek for more.

Together, we create a blaze,
A legacy of hope to raise.
From cinders grand, we shine so bright,
Transcending all into the light.

Whirls of Transformation

In a world that spins and sways,
Change unfolds in endless ways.
With every turn, a chance to grow,
In whirls of life, we come to know.

Colors shift beneath our feet,
Moments fleeting, bittersweet.
Through the chaos, we embrace,
For transformation finds its place.

As seasons change, we rise and fall,
In the dance of life, we hear the call.
With every fall, a chance to fly,
In the spiral, we learn to try.

Heartbeats echo in the flow,
Lessons learned, seeds we sow.
Through the storms and sunny skies,
In whirls of change, our spirit flies.

Embrace the twists, the turns, the bends,
For in these moments, our journey blends.
Transformation is our sacred art,
In every ending, a new start.

The Resilient Flame

In the dark, a flicker glows,
Silent strength in warmth it shows.
Against the winds that howl and bite,
The resilient flame burns ever bright.

Through storms that come, and shadows cast,
It stands its ground, steadfast and fast.
With every wave, it bends, won't break,
A beacon bold for hope's sweet sake.

Embers dance in the cool night air,
Whispers of dreams linger everywhere.
Each spark a story, each glow a fight,
The resilient flame ignites the night.

When darkness looms and fear draws nigh,
The flame persists, it will not die.
For in its heart, a truth remains:
Life's battles fought, but courage gains.

So gather 'round this flickering light,
Let it warm your soul, guide your sight.
From small beginnings, greatness grows,
The resilient flame forever glows.

Dance of the Rising

In the dawn, the colors blend,
Softly waking, night's friend.
The sun ascends, a golden sphere,
A dance begins, as day draws near.

From hills and valleys, shadows flee,
Nature's pulse, a symphony.
With every note, the world inspires,
The dance of life, with dreams afire.

Petals open to the skies,
In gentle movements, beauty lies.
Each breeze a partner, twirls and spins,
The dance of joy that never ends.

As morning light bathes every face,
We join together in this space.
With hearts aligned, we lift and soar,
In the dance of the rising, forevermore.

So let us sway to life's embrace,
In every step, find sacred grace.
For in each moment, a chance to sing,
The dance of the rising, our spirits bring.

Hopes Amidst the Ashes

In the ruins where shadows lie,
Beneath the sky, remnants sigh.
Yet from the dust, a seed takes root,
Hopes amidst the ashes, resolute.

In the silence, a whisper stirs,
Soft resilience in gentle purrs.
Through despair, a new path grows,
Hopes flicker bright, like springtime's rose.

Each heart a flame, ignites the dark,
A sacred promise, a tiny spark.
Together we rise, hand in hand,
From ashes born, we take a stand.

So let us gather, share our dreams,
In strength united, nothing seems.
For in the wreckage, beauty thrives,
Hopes amidst the ashes, love survives.

With every tear, a clearer view,
The dawn awakens, fresh and new.
From shattered past, a future gleams,
Hopes amidst the ashes, we weave our dreams.

Songs of the Ashen Sky

In twilight's glow, the silence sings,
Across the sky, what beauty brings?
With ashen hues that softly glow,
Songs of the ashen sky flow slow.

The clouds gather, a canvas gray,
Each whisper echoing what we say.
In shadows cast by evening's breath,
An anthem rises, defying death.

With tender notes, they weave their tale,
A melody where dreams prevail.
Through loss, through pain, our voices soar,
Songs of the ashen sky restore.

As stars awaken, we find our peace,
In cosmic rhythms, heartbeats cease.
A harmony blends with night's embrace,
In songs of the ashen sky, we trace.

So listen closely, hear the sound,
In every heartbeat, life is found.
For in each song, the echoes lie,
The timeless rhythm of the ashen sky.

Spirit of the Reborn

From ashes, new wings unfurl,
A gentle whisper in the swirl,
In twilight's embrace, hope will soar,
Awakened hearts seek evermore.

Through trials deep, the shadows tread,
A dance of light where dreams are fed,
With every tear, the soul refines,
The spirit lives, and love entwines.

In the silence, strength does grow,
A testament to all we know,
With every breath, a promise speaks,
The path ahead, though winding, peaks.

As morning breaks, we rise anew,
United, strong, our spirits true,
Embrace the journey, feel the grace,
In rebirth's light, find our place.

Each heartbeat sings a sacred tune,
A symphony beneath the moon,
Together we tread, no fear to mourn,
In every soul, the spirit's reborn.

Dreams in the Firelight

Beneath the stars, a flicker bright,
Whispers of dreams ignite the night,
In shadows cast, our hopes take flight,
Bound by the warmth of firelight.

With each crackle, visions dance,
A rhythm leads us, lost in trance,
The world fades out, a daring chance,
In flames we find our wild romance.

The stories shared, the laughter bright,
In every glow, we reunite,
Around this flame, hearts feel so light,
Together we chase our pure delight.

The embers whisper secrets old,
In intimate stories, dreams retold,
As firelight wraps us, brave and bold,
In these moments, true love unfolds.

So hold this warmth, let spirits ride,
In every spark, we find our guide,
Embrace the night, with hearts open wide,
In dreams of firelight, we abide.

Flickering Resilience

Amidst the storms, a flicker glows,
In darkest nights, the spirit grows,
With every trial, the strength it shows,
Resilience blooms, as courage flows.

Through winds that howl, and shadows fall,
A steadfast heart stands brave and tall,
With every setback, we heed the call,
In flickering light, we will not stall.

Against the waves, we stand our ground,
In unity, our power found,
With every heartbeat, a promise crowned,
Resilience whispers all around.

When hope seems lost, and paths unclear,
Look to the light, let go of fear,
In moments brief, find strength to steer,
Flickering flames, forever near.

So cherish the glow, let it ignite,
A beacon of love in the night,
Together we'll rise, reaching the height,
In flickering resilience, pure delight.

Flames of the Eternal

In the silence of the night to see,
A flickering flame, wild and free,
It dances slow, a sacred plea,
In flames of the eternal, we will be.

Through war and peace, the embers glow,
A timeless story weaves its flow,
With every spark, our spirits grow,
To sustain the fire, we'll bestow.

When shadows loom, the warmth remains,
An ancient call through joy and pains,
In unity, our love sustains,
Through every challenge, light remains.

So gather close, let fears depart,
With flames of love that fill each heart,
In the ember's grasp, we play our part,
Eternal fire, never to part.

In the glow, our souls take flight,
Bound by the dance of day and night,
In flames of eternal, pure and bright,
Together we shine, a radiant light.

Awakening from the Ashes

From darkness deep, I rise anew,
With hope ignited, a vibrant hue.
Shattered pieces find their place,
In the warmth of love's embrace.

Through the embers, I walk tall,
Each step taken, I heed the call.
What once was lost, now shines bright,
A phoenix soaring into the light.

With scars adorned like badges worn,
A testament to battles sworn.
In the whispering winds I hear,
The song of life, so sweet and clear.

Nature's gifts, they gently grace,
The journey etched on life's vast face.
In every heartbeat, truth resides,
Awakening the soul that hides.

So let the past in flames dissolve,
Into the now, our hearts evolve.
From ashes rising, bold and free,
We find our strength, our destiny.

The Soul's Flamenco

In rhythm's pulse, the spirit sways,
With every beat, the heart obeys.
Feet in motion, passion's flame,
Dancing wild, we call your name.

Fingers snap as shadows twirl,
Each moment spins, a vibrant whirl.
Underneath the starry sky,
The soul's flamenco, spirits fly.

With every step, a story told,
Of love and laughter, brave and bold.
A tapestry of dreams and thirst,
In every turn, the soul immersed.

Voices rise like waves of sound,
In this embrace, we are unbound.
The dance carries us, medicine sweet,
Where every heart and dream can meet.

So let us twirl 'neath the moonlight's gleam,
In this dance, we find our dream.
The rhythm calls, the night is ours,
In the soul's flamenco, we find stars.

Visions in the Firelight

In the flicker of flames, shadows play,
Whispers of stories, night turns to day.
Eyes reflecting the burning glow,
Visions emerge from the depths below.

Echoes of laughter, memories shared,
In this sacred space, hearts are bared.
A gathering bright, love intertwined,
In the firelight, our souls aligned.

Every spark a fleeting light,
Chasing dreams into the night.
Fire's warmth, our spirits rise,
With every ember, the past defies.

As the stars above start to gleam,
We bask together, lost in dream.
The flickering dance, so wild, so free,
In the firelight, we find our glee.

So let the flames guide our way,
In their embrace, we choose to stay.
Visions invoked, luminous and bright,
In the firelight, we take flight.

Dance of Liberation

With arms outstretched, we free the soul,
In this dance, we become whole.
Shaking off the weight of fears,
Each movement flowing through our years.

The music calls, we take a chance,
Embracing life in this wild dance.
To breathe, to laugh, to truly see,
In this rhythm, we find the key.

Every twist, each turn we take,
A breaking point, a chance to wake.
We shed the chains that held us tight,
In the dance of liberation, we ignite.

With every heartbeat, courage grows,
The spirit blooms, and love bestows.
We twirl into the boundless air,
A celebration of joy laid bare.

And so we dance, and so we sing,
In our hearts, the freedom brings.
Together strong, we'll chart our fate,
In the dance of liberation, we celebrate.

Battle of the Embers

In shadows deep, the flames arise,
Warriors clash beneath dark skies.
Ashes fall like whispers sweet,
Dancing softly with defeat.

In the night, their spirit glows,
Fighting hard, the courage flows.
Wildfire's roar and ember's flight,
Echo fierce throughout the night.

With every spark, a heart ignites,
Battles waged through endless nights.
Among the smoke, the truth is found,
When strength in unity is bound.

Time stands still as echoes fade,
Memories forged of light and shade.
Heroes rise from fiery lore,
With burning hearts they seek for more.

The battle ends, but embers stay,
A silent pledge to find the way.
From ashes new, the stories bloom,
In every heart, there's room for gloom.

The Luminary's Path

A glow appears on distant hills,
Guiding souls through quiet thrills.
Every step a tale retold,
Of dreams and hopes, both brave and bold.

The moonlit whispers carve the night,
Gifts of wisdom, pure and bright.
In shadows cast by ancient trees,
The path unravels with the breeze.

Stars above like diamonds gleam,
Illuminating every dream.
Footprints left in earth and stone,
Sow seeds of courage, never alone.

With every turn, the heart seeks light,
Through tangled woods and tranquil flight.
Underneath the canopy's sway,
A luminary guides the way.

And as the dawn begins to break,
New paths appear with every wake.
In morning's glow, we find our part,
With luminaries in our heart.

Spirit of the Ignited

In flickering flames the spirit lies,
Awakening beneath the skies.
Every heartbeat, a whispering call,
A dance of courage, rise or fall.

The fire stirs, ignites the soul,
Passion's warmth makes the broken whole.
Within the blaze, the shadows break,
Transforming pain for freedom's sake.

From fiery depths, the spirit soars,
Breaking free from self-made doors.
Through trials faced, the journey shared,
In every spark, the heart declared.

The night may hold its darker shades,
Yet in the dawn, the light invades.
Empowered by the flames we trust,
To rise, to shine, to spark the just.

In unity, the embers breathe,
As hope ignites, we dare believe.
With fervent hearts, we stand aligned,
As spirits bright, no fear confined.

Ashes Cradled in Celestial Wings

In twilight's grasp, the ashes glow,
Whispers of dreams in the afterflow,
Carried by winds that softly sing,
Cascades of hope on celestial wing.

From the earth, they rise with grace,
Finding their place in the vast embrace,
Where stardust dances with ancient light,
Transforming shadows into the night.

With every flicker, a story's told,
Of battles fought, of spirits bold,
In silence they soar, free from strife,
Ashes cradle the essence of life.

In cosmic arms, they learn to fly,
Beyond the limits of earth and sky,
Each ember a memory set alight,
In the realm where the stars ignite.

Softly they drift, in rhythms divine,
Echoes of laughter, of love entwined,
Forever cherished, these embers bright,
In the vast expanse of the endless night.

Beats of a Forgotten Fury

In shadows deep, a heart does pound,
Echoes of anger, an ancient sound,
Lost in the silence of tales untold,
Yearning for warmth in the bitter cold.

Fury ignites in the darkened corner,
Awakens the spirits of forgotten mourners,
With every beat, a promise made,
A pulse of hope where shadows fade.

In whispered winds, the anger swells,
Rumbling forth like distant bells,
An anthem rising from tales of old,
Beats of a fury, fierce and bold.

Chained by the echoes of what remains,
Yet breaking free through the silent pains,
In symphonies layered, the heart reflects,
A forgotten fury that time protects.

With every breath, a surge of fire,
The rhythm speaks of deep desire,
From ashes formed, a legacy wakes,
In the dance of anger, the heart quakes.

From Cinders to Celestial Skies

From cinders low, a spark will rise,
Igniting hope beneath dark skies,
Embers dance in the twilight air,
Crafting dreams with tender care.

As flames anew begin to swell,
They whisper secrets no tongue can tell,
In swirling flames, the shadows part,
Guiding the way to a hopeful heart.

With each flicker, a journey starts,
Releasing burdens, unchained hearts,
From ashes past, we carve our way,
Toward brighter dawns, a new display.

Celestial skies in an endless sweep,
A tapestry woven, souls to keep,
From cinders born, a tapestry spun,
Under the gaze of the radiant sun.

Flowing onward, like rivers vast,
We carry the light, embracing the past,
From cinders to skies, a legacy flies,
In the warmth of love, true freedom lies.

Harmony of the Resilient Heart

In whispers soft, the heart takes flight,
Carving through darkness, embracing light,
With every beat, a story unfolds,
In the tapestry woven with threads of gold.

Resilience blooms in the face of strife,
Crafting beauty from the shards of life,
A melody soaring, fierce and free,
A harmony birthed from agony.

Bound by love and stitched with pain,
The heart finds strength in the pouring rain,
In echoes sweet, the spirit grows,
Through storms and tempests, the true self shows.

Every fracture, a note in the song,
Crafting a symphony where souls belong,
With rhythms of hope and dreams that start,
We dance to the tunes of the resilient heart.

In unity forged, we rise above,
In the weaving of faith and boundless love,
Together we sing, our voices part,
In the harmony of the resilient heart.

Dreams of the Flame-Forged

In twilight's whisper, embers glow,
A forge of dreams, they ebb and flow.
Hearts shaped by fire, fierce and bright,
In the depths of night, they spark with light.

From ashes rise, a phoenix born,
In every battle, weary, worn.
Yet courage fuels the flame within,
To rise once more, to wear the skin.

Together bound, through trials we tread,
With fiery passion, never dread.
For every dream we dare to chase,
Is crafted strong, by time and grace.

Stars align, the vision clear,
Through burning paths, we persevere.
Each flicker, each blaze, ignites the night,
Our spirits soared, like kites in flight.

The flame-forged hearts will ever shine,
In unity, we intertwine.
With dreams aflame, we face the storm,
With love and hope, our souls transform.

The Resurgence of Radiance

In shadows deep, a glow emerges,
A whisper soft, the heartenge surges.
From silent depths, light starts to creep,
Awakening the dreams we keep.

The dawn ascends, a canvas bright,
With strokes of gold, dispelling night.
With every breath, the world anew,
Our spirits dance, as hope breaks through.

Through trials faced, and storms endured,
Our inner flames have been assured.
In radiant hues, we find our place,
In every smile, in every trace.

Together we rise, hand in hand,
As light ignites across the land.
United we shine, a force of grace,
In the resurgence, we find our space.

As sunsets fade, our hearts will roam,
In realms of light, we've found our home.
With every dawn, a chance to bloom,
In the radiance, forever loom.

Tides of Transformation

The ocean's call, a siren's song,
With every wave, we flow along.
In ebb and flow, the lessons clear,
Transformation waits, we have no fear.

A tide of change, relentless force,
Guiding hearts upon their course.
With every surge, we rise and fall,
In unity, we answer the call.

The storms may roar, the skies may gray,
Yet in our hearts, hope lights the way.
Each tidal wave, a cleansing breath,
In change, we find a dance with death.

From grains of sand, we shape our path,
Embracing joy, we seek the math.
With every tide, the world anew,
Transformation's grace, a vibrant hue.

Together we flow, as rivers meet,
In currents strong, our hearts compete.
With every surge, we rise above,
In tides of change, we find our love.

A Fire Within

In quiet moments, embers gleam,
A flicker soft, beyond the dream.
With whispered thoughts, ignite the spark,
A fire within that lights the dark.

Through trials faced and fears released,
With every breath, the flame increased.
It roars alive, a passion strong,
In harmony, we find our song.

Against the cold and bitter wind,
This inner blaze, our hearts defend.
With courage bright, we stand as one,
In fires of hope, we've just begun.

From ashes rise, unchained, free,
This fire within, it speaks to me.
In every heartbeat, truths collide,
In warmth and light, we will abide.

Together we fuel this radiant glow,
A fire within, forever flow.
With dreams afire, we claim the night,
In flames of love, we find our light.

Heartbeat of the Flame

In the quiet night, whispers stir,
Flickering shadows dance and blur.
Each spark a dream that yearns to rise,
Embers glow under starry skies.

Passion pulses in the dark,
Fueling the soul, igniting a spark.
Fear fades like morning mist,
In the heart of hope, we persist.

Golden hues wrap around the night,
Casting warmth in the soft twilight.
With every heartbeat, life proclaims,
The fire within is never tamed.

When storms rage and winds howl,
The flame stands fierce, the heart will growl.
In every flicker, there's a chance,
To rise anew, to learn the dance.

Burning bright, our spirits soar,
With every challenge, we seek for more.
Together we face the night's embrace,
In the heartbeat of the flame, we find our place.

Chasing the Horizon

Out where the sun meets the endless sea,
Waves whisper secrets of infinity.
Footprints fade in the golden sand,
Dreams stretch wide, just like our plans.

Each dawn uncovers a new embrace,
Life's a journey, a thrilling race.
With eyes on the skyline, hearts entwined,
We chase the horizon, paths aligned.

Clouds like cotton dance in the blue,
Each one a canvas for dreams to pursue.
We run with laughter, unbound and wild,
Nature cradles us, free as a child.

Every sunset tells tales untold,
Lessons learned, a sight to behold.
In twilight's glow, our spirits shine,
Chasing the horizon, yours and mine.

With every heartbeat, hope renews,
Paths diverge, but our choice we choose.
Forever wandering, yet never lost,
In chasing horizons, we count the cost.

Soul's Renaissance

In the ruins of yesterday's pain,
New growth rises, like joy from rain.
Painted skies fill with dreams anew,
Whispers of life that once withdrew.

Each heartbeat echoes, a gentle call,
Reminding us that we can stand tall.
With every brush of hopeful light,
We sing with the stars, embracing the night.

Fact and fiction weave a tale,
Of breaking chains where spirits sail.
Awakening within, a fire ignites,
A dance begins in the newfound heights.

Through shadows cast, we learn to soar,
Beyond the darkness, we find our core.
A renaissance born from ashes' embrace,
In the depths of our souls, we find grace.

Together we rise, like dawn above,
In the heart's tapestry, we weave love.
For every struggle, there's peace in sight,
In the soul's renaissance, we shine bright.

Rhapsody of the Luminous

Stars shimmer in the velvet night,
Their glow a promise, pure delight.
Like distant whispers, they sing and sway,
In harmony, they light our way.

Each twinkling dance, a tale to share,
Of love and loss, of dreams laid bare.
They guide our hearts, soft and true,
In the rhapsody of the luminous view.

Moonlit dreams float on the breeze,
Every heartbeat blends with trees.
Awake at night, we find our truth,
In every shadow, flows vibrant youth.

With every glance, the cosmos sings,
Tales of hope and the joy it brings.
Unified in bliss, the night we claim,
In the rhapsody of the luminous flame.

Together we twirl under celestial lights,
Holding on, through endless flights.
In the night sky, our spirits hum,
In the rhapsody of light, we become one.

Wings of Eternal Hope

In quiet corners of the night,
A whisper stirs the fading light.
The dreams take flight on gentle winds,
As hearts embrace what hope begins.

With every dawn, a promise clear,
To chase away all doubt and fear.
The sun will rise, our spirits soar,
For each new day, we yearn for more.

Through trials faced, we find our way,
The light will guide, won't lead astray.
For every path that bends and breaks,
A new chance blooms, a love awakes.

With wings of faith, we lift our eyes,
To catch the colors of the skies.
In every step, a dance of grace,
Together we will find our place.

Our hearts a canvas, bright and bold,
With stories shared, and tales retold.
In unity, our dreams combine,
In hope's warm glow, our spirits shine.

Celestial Uprising

Stars ignite the darkened veil,
Their shimmer tells a timeless tale.
In endless night, the silence breaks,
Awakening what stillness wakes.

Galaxies swirl in a cosmic dance,
While distant worlds invite a chance.
With every pulse of radiant light,
The heavens whisper, 'Take your flight.'

In dreams that spiral, soaring high,
We find the strength to reach the sky.
Through storms of doubt, we chart our course,
With every heartbeat, we find the source.

As comets blaze with fiery trails,
We lift our hearts, and fear unveils.
The universe in all its grace,
Encourages us to embrace.

Together we, in stars entwined,
With visions bold, our souls aligned.
In every rise, a spark ignites,
A celestial dance, our shared delights.

The Dance of Fire and Flight

In twilight's glow, the embers play,
As shadows stretch and fade away.
The flames, they leap, a vibrant sight,
In this embrace of fire and flight.

With every flicker, passion's spark,
Illuminates the coming dark.
We weave our dreams in fiery strands,
And forge our fate with tender hands.

The winds will whisper in the night,
As we twirl 'neath the silver light.
In every gasp, a breath of heat,
The dance of souls, a rhythmic beat.

With hearts ablaze, we spin and sway,
In love's embrace, come what may.
As flames consume what once was known,
We rise anew, no longer alone.

In every turn, our spirits soar,
With fiery grace, we both explore.
Together lost in passion's flight,
As shadows fade, we claim the night.

Vows of the Reborn

From ashes rise, a brand new start,
With open wings and weary hearts.
We cast aside the weight of despair,
In vows of love, a bond to share.

Through trials faced, we intertwine,
With strength to guide, our spirits shine.
In every promise, hope ignites,
To light the way through darkest nights.

The past is but a fleeting ghost,
We cherish now, we hold it close.
In every tear that bathes the ground,
A fertile soil, where love is found.

With gentle whispers, truths unfold,
In stories shared, our hearts are bold.
Each vow we make, a sacred flame,
To seal our bond, forever claim.

No longer bound by chains of old,
The future bright, the stories told.
With every breath, a new refrain,
In unity, we rise again.

A Symphony of Rebirth

In the morning light, fresh blooms rise,
Nature sings sweetly, painting the skies.
Whispers of hope in every soft breeze,
Life reawakens with effortless ease.

Streams of silver flow, gently they weave,
Through valleys of green, where dreams believe.
Birds take to wing, in joyous flight,
A symphony starts, framed in pure light.

Each heartbeat echoes, a rhythm so true,
Colors burst forth, with every dew.
The world spins anew, life's dance unfurls,
A vibrant tapestry, reflecting our pearls.

In shadows of doubt, the dawn breaks clear,
Every moment cherished, each breath sincere.
Roots intertwine, in the soil they thrive,
A celebration of stories, where all are alive.

From the depths of night, to the dawn's embrace,
Rebirth is a journey, transcending all space.
Together we rise, like the sun's endless climb,
In this symphony grand, we dance into time.

The Rekindled Spirit

In the ashes of sorrow, a spark ignites,
Flickering softly, with whispers of light.
From shadows we emerge, renewed and bold,
A rekindled spirit, breaking the mold.

With every heartbeat, courage reclaims,
The fire inside, no more hidden flames.
We stand together, voices entwined,
Breathing in strength, leaving fears behind.

Through tempest and storm, we find our way,
With faith as our guide, come what may.
Each setback a lesson, a chance to shine,
In the face of the night, our spirits align.

Like phoenixes rising, we reach for the skies,
As embers of hope abruptly arise.
The world is our canvas, painted in dreams,
In the dance of rebirth, nothing's as it seems.

With laughter and love, we light up the dark,
In unity's glow, we find our spark.
The journey continues, never apart,
Forever ignited, the rekindled heart.

Heartstrings of Flame

Strummed softly on strings, a melody so bright,
Fires that connect us, in day and night.
Each note a heartbeat, weaving through time,
A song of our souls, in harmonious rhyme.

In the flickering glow, our passions arise,
Heat of desire, igniting the skies.
With every deep breath, we shatter the chains,
Releasing the echoes, love's sweet refrains.

Around the warm hearth, stories find light,
In shadows of doubt, we stand up and fight.
Through struggles and triumphs, we dance with grace,
Heartstrings of flame, in this sacred space.

With laughter and tears, we blend joy and pain,
In the tapestry woven, what love can sustain.
Each moment a gift, a bond that we claim,
Forever entwined, in heartstrings of flame.

As the embers glow softly, we know it's our truth,
In the warmth of connection, we find our youth.
Together we rise, igniting our fate,
A symphony played, never too late.

From Ash to Aura

In silence we fall, to ashes we yield,
Yet deep in our souls, new energy swelled.
From embers of past, a bright future flows,
Transforming the pain, as wisdom bestows.

The essence of life, vibrant and bold,
Glistening softly, like treasures untold.
From shadows we step, unchained and free,
Embracing our journey, in awe of what's to be.

With each sunrise, the world starts anew,
Casting off burdens, in shades of deep blue.
Our spirits ignite, like stars in the night,
From ash to aura, we're guided by light.

In the dance of existence, we find our way,
Turning heartache to hope, come what may.
With courage as armor, we shift and we sway,
From ash to aura, forever we stay.

In the tapestry woven, our stories unite,
Emerging from darkness, we blossom in light.
With every step forward, a promise we make,
From ash to aura, our hearts never break.

Hymn of the Inextinguishable

In shadows deep, a spark will glow,
Resilient heart, against the flow.
With every trial, strength will rise,
In darkness found, the spirit flies.

A whisper calls, a silent plea,
Awakening the soul set free.
No storm can break what's built to last,
In every breath, the echo's vast.

We march as one, through fire and strain,
With every step, we bear the pain.
Together forged, in love and light,
An anthem born, to greet the night.

The flame persists, it cannot fade,
With hope as guide, the path is laid.
Through trials faced, we gather strength,
In unity, we find our length.

So sing we now, our voices high,
In harmony, we reach the sky.
Inextinguishable, we remain,
Through every joy, and every pain.

The Rise of the Radiant Soul

Awake in light, the soul will rise,
With dawn's embrace, to claim the skies.
A spark ignites, the heart beats bold,
With dreams of youth, a sight to hold.

In every trial, a lesson learned,
With passion's fire, the spirit burned.
The journey flows, like rivers wide,
In every wave, the truths confide.

Through mountains high, the echoes call,
And in their whispers, we stand tall.
The radiant light, we feel it glow,
In every heart, the hope we sow.

With every step on this great quest,
We find within, our truest best.
The rise is now, it can't be stopped,
In unity, our spirits hopped.

A dance of light, a tapestry,
Woven with dreams, our legacy.
As one we shine, bright in the whole,
Together we rise, the radiant soul.

Transformation in the Blaze

In flames of change, the old must fade,
Through ash and smoke, new paths are laid.
With courage fierce, we face the fire,
In every spark, ignites desire.

From ember low, to brighter dawn,
A metamorphosis, reborn.
With every challenge, strength is found,
In blazing light, we gather round.

The dance of time, a swirling glow,
In the heart's rhythm, we learn to flow.
Embrace the heat, let fears take flight,
In transformation, we claim our light.

Beyond the flame, a vision clear,
The journey calls, we have no fear.
With every step, the world unfolds,
A story rich, in dreams retold.

So rise from ashes, feel the grace,
In every moment, we find our place.
In the blaze, we see the way,
Transformed anew, we greet the day.

Wings Against the Wind

With outstretched wings, we dare to fly,
Against the storm, we touch the sky.
The winds may howl, but hearts are strong,
In every challenge, we belong.

Through gusts and gales, we learn to soar,
With every struggle, we're wanting more.
The heights we reach, the dreams we chase,
In every flight, we find our place.

Each feather's weight, a tale to tell,
In letting go, we rise so well.
The skies are vast, with clouds that spin,
Through storms we breach, to find within.

So take a breath, embrace the strain,
Unfold your wings, let go of pain.
With hope as guide, we'll chart the seas,
In every wind, we feel the breeze.

For every gust that pushes back,
We find a strength, we won't lack.
With wings unfurled, we'll rise above,
In fierce embrace, we find our love.

The Alchemy of Heat and Hope

In the furnace of dreams, we ignite,
Crafting visions in the shimmering night.
Each spark whispers tales of desire,
A dance of shadows, a flicker of fire.

Heat and hope entwined in embrace,
Transforming lives with a radiant grace.
From the ashes of fears, new worlds are spun,
Melding darkness to light, we rise as one.

Hands reach out through the searing haze,
Embers of courage ignite the blaze.
Through trials and tests, we find our way,
With warmth in our hearts, we'll not go astray.

Every breath breaths life into the flame,
A testament bold, with no one to blame.
In the alchemy of heart, we'll thrive,
Where hope and heat shall keep dreams alive.

Together we stand, unyielding and strong,
In the heat of the moment, we all belong.
With hope as our guide, and fire our song,
In harmony's rhythm, we shall dance along.

Whirlwinds of the Fiery Soul

Spirited whirlwinds within our core,
Fiery tempests that endlessly soar.
With every pulse, the struggle ignites,
A wild dance of our passionate fights.

In the heart's eye, the chaos unfurl,
Each twist and turn, a vibrant swirl.
Echoes of courage, fierce and bold,
In the depths of our being, the fervor is gold.

Through storms of doubt, we march ahead,
With fiery resolve, our spirits are fed.
The soul's essence, ablaze in the night,
A beacon of strength, glowing so bright.

From the ashes of fear, we rise and we learn,
In the fires of life, our souls start to burn.
Embracing the chaos, we dance with fate,
In the whirlwinds of passion, we celebrate.

Together we soar on the winds of the flame,
A chorus of voices, no two are the same.
In this whirlwind of spirit, we stand tall,
Fiery souls united, we conquer all.

The Glimmer Beyond the Ashen Veil

Beneath the ashes, a light starts to gleam,
A glimmer of hope in the starlit dream.
With every shadow that tries to enthrall,
The spark of our spirit still answers the call.

Veils of despair may cloud the view,
Yet within, a promise, pure and true.
Each flicker reminds us to rise from the depths,
To find our own voice in the whispered breaths.

As embers linger in the cool night air,
We seek the warmth; we foster, we care.
Beyond the veil, a vision awaits,
A tapestry woven with love on our plates.

Through trials and tears, we find our way,
Dancing in rhythm, come what may.
The glimmer reminds us in times of fight,
A heart filled with fire will always bring light.

Together we journey, united we stand,
Embracing the journey, hand in hand.
For beyond the ashes, in twilight's embrace,
The glimmer of hope shall forever hold grace.

The Lament of Fiery Echoes

In the silence, echoes of fire reside,
The lament of hearts, where passions collide.
In whispers of flame, we feel the sting,
The sorrows of longing, a bittersweet ring.

Fleeting moments, like embers they fade,
Each memory a song, in shadows we wade.
Lost in the echoes, our spirits take flight,
The dance of the fire ignites through the night.

Yet in the lament, resilience will grow,
From ashes of sorrow, the strength we bestow.
Through trials and heartaches, we carve our own way,
In the echoes of flame, we learn how to stay.

With each fiery note, we rise and we fall,
The symphony plays as it beckons us all.
In the depths of the night, we find unity,
A chorus of spirits ignites a decree.

Together in sorrow, we carry the weight,
With fire in our souls, we embrace our fate.
For in every lament, together we find,
The echoes of fire forever entwined.

Whispers of the Ascending Flame

In twilight's embrace, a glow ignites,
Soft whispers dance with the stars at night.
Each flicker tells of dreams alive,
Carried forth on winds that strive.

Silhouettes sway in the gentle breeze,
Echo of warmth through ancient trees.
The flame ascends, a flickering sigh,
Awakening hope beneath the sky.

Through shadows deep, a luminescent trail,
Guiding souls where the heart won't fail.
In fragile light, we find our way,
As whispers cloak the break of day.

From ashes past, new tales arise,
With every spark, a chance to fly.
The rising flame, a promise sworn,
In whispered truths, we are reborn.

The nightingale sings to the hunger of night,
As embers dance in transformative flight.
Together we rise, intertwined by fate,
In whispers of love, we celebrate.

Resonance of the Reborn Spirit

A heartbeat echoes through the silent land,
Awakening dreams long buried in sand.
The spirit stirs, igniting the dawn,
From the ashes of dusk, a new life is drawn.

In the stillness, the universe hums,
Each note a promise, as morning comes.
Rebirth whispers in the vibrant air,
In every moment, the bold and the rare.

It travels through valleys, over hills wide,
Where the lost find their compass, nowhere to hide.
A melody sweet with a hint of the past,
A resonance bold, built to last.

Through storms and shadows, we gather the light,
A chorus of souls, ready to fight.
Together we rise, voices combined,
In the resonance found, the truth defined.

With every heartbeat, a new story spun,
In the afterglow where life has begun.
A dance of spirits in the expansive sphere,
In the resonance of love, forever near.

The Soul's Embers in Flight

Deep in the night, embers glow bright,
A dance of the souls taking flight.
With every spark, a whispering call,
Tales of the past, inspiring all.

Through smoky tendrils, the stories weave,
Of journeys old and dreams to believe.
Together we soar, unbound by the past,
In radiant light, our hearts beat fast.

Above the horizon where shadows fall,
The embers rise, inviting us all.
Each flicker a promise, each spark a trace,
Of hope and love in this vast, open space.

In the twilight's glow, the spirits entwine,
A symphony sweet, an echo divine.
As the soul's embers flicker and gleam,
We dance through the night, igniting the dream.

With wings made of fire, we glide and we soar,
On the winds of our past, we forever explore.
In the embrace of the night, we take flight,
The soul's embers burning, forever alight.

Songs of the Rising Ashes

From ashes we rise, a symphony bold,
With melodies rich and stories untold.
Each note a flicker, a heartbeat anew,
In the dance of rebirth, we find what is true.

The echoes of fire, once lost in the night,
Now weave through the air, a delicate light.
In the stillness, a song softly plays,
A chorus of hope in the brightening days.

With grace we revive, in harmony bound,
The spirit of life in each moment found.
Together, we sing of our journeys ahead,
In songs of the rising, where dreams are fed.

Fires burn low, yet the light will persist,
In the hearts of the brave, in the fog of the mist.
Through every challenge, we stand and we sway,
In the songs of the ashes that guide our way.

As the dawn approaches with colors ablaze,
We gather our strength in a wondrous haze.
With voices united, through trials and throngs,
We celebrate life in the songs that belong.

Radiance After Darkness

In the night so deep, we find our way,
Stars whisper softly, guiding the stray.
Once shadows loomed, despair took flight,
Now dawn breaks bright, banishing night.

A flicker of hope, igniting the soul,
With each passing moment, we start to unroll.
The past may linger, but light pulls us near,
Filling our hearts with warmth, not fear.

Through trials we walk, hand in hand,
Together we rise, like grains of sand.
Emerging anew, from depths we restore,
Boundless our spirits, forever we soar.

Golden horizons stretch wider each day,
Chasing the shadows that fade away.
With every heartbeat, a promise we keep,
In the light of our love, we no longer weep.

Radiant futures await, we embrace,
Filling the void with laughter and grace.
Together as one, through joy and through pain,
We'll shine ever brighter, our hearts like the rain.

The Heart's Resurgence

In silence, it beats, a whisper of fears,
Lost in the echoes, it fights through the years.
But still it awakens, with fervor and fire,
A longing for love, a deep-rooted desire.

Out from the shadows, it rises anew,
With strength like the mountains, steadfast and true.
A symphony played on the strings of the past,
Each note a reminder, that nothing can last.

Through cracks in the armor, emotions break free,
Like rivers of sunlight, cascading the sea.
Transforming the pain into beauty untold,
Restoring the warmth, as the heart finds its gold.

The heart's resurgence in the light of the dawn,
No longer a prisoner, the chains gently gone.
With grace it will dance, in the rhythm of time,
Embracing that life is a journey in rhyme.

With every heartbeat, a new chapter starts,
In the book of existence, where love paints the arts.
So let it be known, through all life's demands,
The heart's resurgence forever expands.

Embers in the Mist

Beneath the fog, where shadows entwine,
Glow little embers, quietly shine.
In whispers of twilight, they flicker and dance,
Holding the secrets of fate's gentle chance.

With each breath of wind, their warmth comes alive,
A promise of hope, where dreams will survive.
Though darkness is thick, and the night feels so long,
Embers keep burning, fervent and strong.

They guide lost souls on their wander to home,
In gardens of promise, no longer to roam.
From ashes of yesterday, life begins bright,
Each spark represents the triumph of light.

The mist may obscure, but can never consume,
The fire within, that lovingly blooms.
So cherish the embers, that light up the vast,
For in every glow, lies a story amassed.

A tapestry woven, with threads full of grace,
Warming the heart in this magical space.
Together we gather, as embers unite,
In the mist we find, our soul's true delight.

Wings of Renewal

With every sunrise, a fresh start bestowed,
Breaking the silence, as new life is sowed.
Wings stretch wide, catching the morning breeze,
Inspiration flows, with the rustle of trees.

Through trials endured, and battles we share,
Our spirits take flight, light, free from despair.
From ashes of yesterday, we rise and take wing,
Embracing our journey, the joy that it brings.

Each feather a story, a mark of our past,
Reminding us gently, that nothing is cast.
With each gentle flap, we soar towards the sky,
Unleashing our dreams, letting our hearts fly.

The winds of change call, in their sweet serenade,
Breathing fresh life into plans once delayed.
Together we embrace, a world yet unseen,
With wings of renewal, we rise like a queen.

So let your heart soar, in this dance of the day,
With love as our compass, we'll find our own way.
In the sky's endless canvas, painted in hue,
Wings of renewal are waiting for you.

The Journey of Embers

In the quiet night sky, stars gleam bright,
Each ember whispers tales of flight.
From ashes we rise, a flickering spark,
Carrying hope through the endless dark.

Guided by dreams, we wander free,
Each heartbeat a dance, a memory.
The path winds on, through valleys wide,
With every step, we cast aside.

In the glow of dusk, shadows appear,
Whispers of past, both distant and near.
Embers ignite, a burning flame,
Reminding us all, we're part of the same.

Through storms of doubt, we brave the night,
In unity's warmth, we find the light.
Together we forge, a brighter way,
With embers in hand, we face the day.

So journey we must, with courage anew,
With each ember's glow, we'll break through.
Transforming the night into morning's grace,
In this journey of embers, we find our place.

Flames of a Forgotten Past

In a world long lost, memories blink,
Flames flicker softly, urging us to think.
Echoes of laughter, whispers of pain,
Remnants of love, like shadows remain.

Burning brightly, in the heart they reside,
Stories untold, we cannot divide.
Through the ashes, our spirits ascend,
To rekindle the bonds that never quite end.

Fires of yesterday, lessons they bring,
Each flicker a song, each burn a sting.
In the warmth of the flame, we learn to endure,
Finding the strength in memories obscure.

As we gaze into the glowing light,
We embrace the past, and hold on tight.
With each crackle, a truth we reclaim,
In flames of a past that still calls our name.

So let us gather, share stories we know,
In the flames of forgotten, together we grow.
For from the ashes, new dreams will rise,
A future ignited beneath endless skies.

Beacons of Resilience

In the darkest moments, we shine like stars,
Beacons of strength, no matter how far.
Each flame a story, a testament tall,
To the power within, we rise above all.

Through trials we face, unyielding we stand,
With embers of courage, we clasp each hand.
In the winds of change, our spirits won't sway,
Lighting the path, come what may.

For in every heart, there's a flicker of fire,
Emboldened in purpose, we rise ever higher.
Together we forge a bond that's unbreakable,
Turning the impossible into the achievable.

Through the echoes of life, our voices unite,
Each flame a whisper; we ignite the night.
With passion as fuel, and hope as our guide,
We carry the torch, through the tempest we ride.

So let our resilience be felt through the storm,
In the warmth of compassion, our hearts stay warm.
As beacons of strength, we illuminate all,
Together in light, we answer the call.

Shadows of the Flame

In the depths of the night, shadows entwine,
Flickering softly, like whispers divine.
A dance of emotions, both sorrow and grace,
In shadows of flame, we find our place.

Each shadow tells stories, of love and of loss,
Tracing the paths that we each have crossed.
In the glow of the embers, the past is alive,
Reminding us gently that we can survive.

For shadows hold power, a lesson in pain,
Through darkness we wander, through sunshine and rain.
In the warmth of the flame, we find comfort and peace,
In shadows we learn that our struggles can cease.

As the night lingers on, we rise from the dark,
With shadows behind us, igniting the spark.
Each flicker a promise that hope is not lost,
In shadows we grow, despite what it costs.

So let us embrace, both the light and the shade,
In the dance of the flame, our spirits won't fade.
For in every shadow, a lesson is gained,
In shadows of flame, our courage is trained.

Chronicles of the Fiery Resurrection

From ashes born, the embers glow,
A tale of strength, through pain we sow.
Each flicker tells of battles fought,
In hearts ablaze, new dreams are sought.

Cinders whisper of hope reborn,
Through shadows deep, a light adorns.
With every flame, the past ignites,
Resilience found in endless nights.

The fire dances, alive and free,
Unfurling wings of destiny.
Together we rise, a radiant crew,
In fiery hues, we start anew.

The blaze within, a guiding star,
Illuminating who we are.
With passion's spark, we claim our fate,
In the chronicle, love resonates.

So let the flames testify our will,
For in this journey, hearts will thrill.
A resurrection fierce and bright,
From darkness blooms a blinding light.

The Ignite and the Infinite

In the silence where shadows play,
A spark awakens the night's ballet.
Waves of energy sway and swirl,
As dreams collide and passions whirl.

The ignite of hope in hearts concealed,
A universe waiting to be revealed.
In every flicker, endless space,
An infinite path we bravely trace.

The fire calls, a siren's song,
In its embrace, we all belong.
From flickers small to roaring flames,
This dance of life, it knows our names.

In every pulse, connection grows,
Through every spark, true love still glows.
Together we venture, hand in hand,
In the infinite, forever we stand.

So let us bask in this divine light,
With souls ignited, spirits in flight.
Through stardust trails and cosmic beams,
We find our truth in whispered dreams.

Spirit's Flame and the Wind's Whisper

The spirit's flame, a gentle blaze,
Brightens the night in a soft haze.
In whispers carried by the breeze,
We dance with nature, hearts at ease.

The wind confides in secrets old,
A tale of warmth, of courage bold.
Through valleys deep, both wide and free,
The flame ignites our unity.

Moments shared beneath the stars,
In laughter and in hidden scars.
With every gust, our fears take flight,
In spirit's glow, we find our light.

So let us breathe the stories near,
As winds embrace, we'll conquer fear.
In harmony, the flames entwine,
With whispers soft, our souls align.

Together, we forge a radiant path,
With spirit's flame, we conquer wrath.
In every heart, a fire burns bright,
Guided by whispers through the night.

Rebirth Amidst the Smoldering Ruins

In ruins deep, where silence falls,
Life murmurs through the crumbling walls.
Amidst the ash, new sprouts arise,
A testament beneath the skies.

The earth remembers, though charred and worn,
From every death, a life is born.
In dusty dreams and fragmented tales,
The soul persists and never pales.

With each dawn's blush, the glow returns,
Igniting hopes and ancient yearns.
In smoldering soil, we plant our seed,
From despair sown, a potent creed.

In unity, we rise once more,
From shattered stones, we seek to soar.
With courage fierce, we face the plight,
Rebirth unfolds in morning light.

So let not fear our hearts consume,
For even in darkness, we find room.
Amidst the ruins, we will stand tall,
In stories etched, we'll never fall.

The Heart That Ignites

In shadows deep, a spark may glow,
A flicker bright in darkest woe.
With whispered hopes, the fire grows,
The heart that ignites, forever flows.

Through trials faced and fears held tight,
It lifts the soul, ignites the night.
With passion's dance, the flame expands,
A warmth that binds with gentle hands.

Each heartbeat drums, a melody,
The rhythm sings of unity.
Together forged through love's sweet art,
In every breath, we feel the heart.

In storms of life where tempests rage,
The heart stands firm, it will not cage.
With courage found in every fight,
It beams with strength, a beacon bright.

So let your spirit rise and thrive,
The heart that ignites keeps hope alive.
In every soul, let passion find,
The flames that kindled love entwined.

Light Beyond the Ashes

From embers cold, a glow persists,
A sign of life that still exists.
Through fire's wrath and time's cruel pass,
There shines a light beyond the ashes.

In desolation, dreams once lost,
We rise again, no matter the cost.
With every tear, a lesson learned,
A flicker bright, our hearts are turned.

Hope finds a way through darkest night,
With every dawn, the future's bright.
From ashes humbled, courage grows,
In every heart, the spirit knows.

Rebuild the world with hands that dare,
To create beauty from despair.
The flames may burn, but won't define,
The light within, forever shine.

So find your strength, let shadows flee,
For there's a light that sets us free.
Through trials faced, we will embrace,
The warmth of life in every place.

Flames in the Abyss

In depths unknown where shadows creep,
The flames in the abyss begin to leap.
They flicker low, then rise so high,
A dance of fire, a fearless cry.

With every spark, they seek to rise,
Illuminating darkened skies.
In swirling depths, they twist and turn,
For every flame, the heart will yearn.

Against the void, a brightness stands,
As hope ignites with steady hands.
In fearsome light, we face our fate,
The flames in the abyss create.

With courage born from deep within,
We embrace the fire, let it begin.
Through trials faced, our spirits soar,
For in the depths, we yearn for more.

So burn, bright flames, and guide the way,
Through shadows deep, we will not sway.
With hearts ablaze, together we fight,
For in the abyss, there shines a light.

Spirit Awakened

In silence deep, a whisper stirs,
The spirit awakened, as time blurs.
With every beat, it calls the soul,
To rise, to shine, to be made whole.

Through journeys vast and lessons learned,
The fires of change in hearts have burned.
With each resolve, new hopes take flight,
The spirit awakened, a guiding light.

In every moment, a chance to grow,
To shed the past and let love flow.
With open hearts, the world we grace,
In unity, we find our place.

So dance with joy, let burdens go,
The spirit awakened, in every glow.
Together strong, through night and day,
We find our path, we light the way.

A journey shared, a vision clear,
The spirit's voice we hold so dear.
In every breath, let life unfold,
With love's embrace, our story's told.

The Blaze That Inspires

From depths of night, a spark will grow,
Illuminating dreams we dare to sow.
With every flame, a story told,
A passion fierce, a heart of gold.

Through storms we rise, together strong,
In unity, we find where we belong.
The fire within ignites our quest,
To chase the light and face the test.

With every breath, new flames arise,
Lighting the path to endless skies.
Through shadows cast, we'll find our way,
In the blaze, our spirits sway.

In quiet moments, embers gleam,
In every heartbeat lies a dream.
Together hand in hand, we'll strive,
With the blaze, we come alive.

From every struggle comes a light,
That fuels our hope, dispels the night.
In every heart, a burning truth,
The blaze that inspires endless youth.

Heart of the Resilient

Through trials faced and battles fought,
A heart beats strong, a lesson taught.
In every bruise, in every fall,
The resilient rise, they heed the call.

With dreams that soar, like wings of grace,
They find the strength in every space.
In tears of joy, and pain, they find,
A heart that knows no bounds or kind.

From ashes born, like phœnix bright,
They stand their ground, a fiery light.
In moments dark, they rise and claim,
The heart of resilient, free of shame.

With every breath, they seek and grow,
Through storms of doubt, their courage flows.
For in the struggle, they hold the key,
To unlock the chains and set them free.

Together we stand, through thick and thin,
With hearts united, we will win.
In strength we trust, our spirits swell,
The heart of the resilient, a sacred spell.

Fiery Reverie

In twilight's glow, the embers dance,
Inviting souls to take a chance.
In dreams ignited, passion's fire,
A reverie of hearts that inspire.

With whispered winds and stars that shine,
We lose ourselves in realms divine.
From shadows deep, our spirits roam,
In fiery visions, we find our home.

Through every dream, the flames entwine,
A tapestry of fate, a sign.
With courage bright, we chase the spark,
Our fiery reverie, against the dark.

In the heat of hope, we rise anew,
In every heartbeat, the fire is true.
With visions bold, our souls ignite,
Creating magic in the night.

As dawn breaks forth, the flames transform,
From fleeting dreams, a lasting norm.
In fiery reverie, we set the pace,
For futures bright, and a warm embrace.

An Anthem for the Reborn

From depths of sorrow, we arise,
With open hearts and fearless eyes.
In every note, an echo sweet,
An anthem sings beneath our feet.

With every dawn, we shed the past,
Embracing light, our shadows cast.
Together strong, we raise our voice,
In unity, we make our choice.

Through trials faced, our spirits soar,
With every heartbeat, we restore.
From ashes cold, a triumph earned,
An anthem played, a fire burned.

With hope as guide, we'll pave the way,
In harmony, we find our sway.
Through every struggle, we stand tall,
In vibrant chorus, we'll never fall.

For every step that we embrace,
Is woven deep in love and grace.
An anthem for the reborn sings,
With joy and peace, our spirit wings.

The Luminous Flame

In the hush of night, it glows,
Dancing shadows, soft and slow.
Whispers of warmth, a gentle glow,
The heart's desire, to love and know.

Flickering bright, it lights the way,
Chasing the dark, keeping fears at bay.
With every spark, dreams take flight,
A beacon of hope in the darkest night.

Each flicker tells a story old,
Of passion fierce, and hearts so bold.
In the twilight, its beauty reigns,
The luminous flame, where love remains.

Through winds that howl, it stands its ground,
In the silence, a soothing sound.
With every breath, it breathes anew,
A timeless dance, forever true.

As it wanes, we hold it tight,
Cherishing the warmth, holding the light.
In every heart, a flame shall stay,
Guiding souls along the way.

Rebirth from Ashes

From ashes deep, a spark takes flight,
In the darkness, emerges light.
Born of struggle, fierce and bold,
A tale of triumph yet untold.

With every tear, a seed is sown,
From desolation, strength has grown.
In the rubble, hope takes root,
Life's sweet song, an ancient lute.

The past may burn, but dreams survive,
In the heart's forge, we feel alive.
Rebirth comes on wings of fire,
Each new dawn, we soar higher.

Emerging from the shadows cast,
A phoenix rises, free at last.
With every step, we forge our fate,
In the cycle of love, we celebrate.

Rebirth from ashes, a powerful grace,
Finding beauty in every trace.
With open arms, we greet the day,
In the light of love, we find our way.

Glory in the Heat

Amidst the flames, we find our might,
In the heat, we shine so bright.
With every pulse, adrenaline flows,
A spirit fierce, as the fire glows.

Battles fought with courage rare,
In the chaos, we find our air.
From trial's forge, our strength is cast,
In glory's name, we rise steadfast.

As embers dance, we hear the call,
In the heart of the blaze, we stand tall.
With fervent hearts, we light the night,
Defying fears, we embrace the fight.

The heat ignites the dreams we chase,
In every struggle, we find our place.
Emboldened souls, forever bold,
In glory's embrace, our stories unfold.

With every heartbeat, we feel the fire,
In the heat of passion, we lift higher.
Embracing life, we carve our art,
In glory of the heat, we find our heart.

The Flame's Lament

In the stillness, a flame does weep,
For dreams lost in the shadows deep.
A flicker dims, once strong and bright,
Now a whisper in the night.

Memories drift like smoke in time,
Each flicker fades, a silent rhyme.
Longing echoes in the breeze,
A heart that yearns, a soul that flees.

As the fire wanes, a tale unwinds,
Of hopes abandoned, of ties that bind.
Yet in the sorrow, beauty blooms,
In the starkness, the heart resumes.

With every sigh, the darkness fades,
Through sorrow's veil, hope still pervades.
For in the loss, new life will start,
The flame's lament, a work of art.

In every end, a new beginning shines,
The flame transforms, as time aligns.
For even as it mourns the night,
The flame will rise, embracing light.

In the Wake of the Flaring Dawn

The sky blushes pink, anew,
Birds stir from nests, take flight,
Whispers of night fade to blue,
Hope flares with the morning light.

Dew-kissed petals, fragrance sweet,
Sunbeams dance on waking grass,
Nature's symphony begins to greet,
In this moment, dreams amass.

Clouds drift like thoughts on the breeze,
Ancient trees sway, roots deep,
Embrace the warmth, feel at ease,
In dawn's magic, secrets keep.

A horizon brushed with gold,
Promises of joy emerge,
Each heartbeat, a tale untold,
In the wake, we're free to surge.

With every ray, shadows retreat,
New beginnings, life expands,
In the wake of hope, we meet,
As the dawn unfolds its hands.

Memories Carried on the Wind

In the hush of twilight's glow,
Whispers dance upon the air,
Echoes of the past that flow,
Stories woven with great care.

Leaves rustle like distant calls,
Each gust recalls a time gone by,
Laughter lingers, joy enthralls,
Truths in the breeze softly sigh.

Old photographs in fading light,
Hold faces that once felt so near,
Through every breeze, a fleeting sight,
In the wind, their voices clear.

Across the fields where shadows play,
Dreams once cherished, softly roam,
Carried far, yet never stray,
In the heart, they find a home.

Memories, like feathers, drift,
Onward through the endless skies,
In every breeze, a gentle gift,
A reminder that love never dies.

Reverberations of a Fabled Revival

In the heart of ancient trees,
Whispers tell of days gone past,
Legends dance on gentle breeze,
Echoes of a spell they cast.

Flickering light from fireflies,
Guides the dreamers through the night,
Beneath the stars, a world that sighs,
Awakens to a hopeful light.

Once forgotten, dreams arise,
From ashes, new life takes its claim,
Each heartbeat writes a grand reprise,
In the dusk, we play the same.

Harmony sings through the night,
Fables weave a thread divine,
Every tale, a spark of light,
In the silence, voices shine.

Revival's kiss on nature's face,
Unites the lost with joy anew,
In reverberations, we embrace,
The magic in a world so true.

The Firebird's Silent Song

In the twilight's tender embrace,
A firebird glides through the air,
With wings unfurled, in radiant grace,
Its silent song beyond compare.

Colors blaze like dreams untold,
Fires of passion burn so bright,
Each feather drips with tales of old,
In the dark, it brings forth light.

Through forests deep and skies so wide,
The firebird paints the night,
In every heart, its flame resides,
Kindling hope, igniting flight.

A whispering breeze speaks its name,
A melody lost, yet still near,
Through hollow echoes, calls the same,
To souls that long to feel the cheer.

In stillness, find the song within,
Let it guide you through the haze,
As the firebird's tales begin,
Embrace the light, ignite your days.

9 781805 618188